THE LOVE AND COMPASSION WORKBOOK

CARLA MINO, M.A.

Printed in the United States of America.

ISBN: 979-8-9860202-5-9 (Paperback)

Front and Back Cover Designed by Carla Mino.

Library of Congress Cataloging - in - Publication Data

Name: Mino, Carla, author
Title: The Love and Compassion Formula
Description: Certificate of Registration. California, 2006

CONTENTS

A NOTE FROM THE AUTHOR

Dear Beautiful Soul,

Welcome to The Love & Compassion Workbook. I'm so grateful you are here.

This workbook is a sacred space to come home to yourself.

If you have landed on these pages, it's likely because your spirit is longing for softness, for truth, and for rest. Perhaps you have been moving through life on autopilot, tending to everyone but yourself, carrying wounds that haven't had time or space to fully breathe. Maybe you have tried to be strong for so long and now you are finally ready to be held.

This workbook was created for women like you. Women on a spiritual journey, walking through burnout, grief, or transition. Yet, still carrying the quiet courage to begin again.

Inside these pages, you will find a gentle formula for healing:

- Connect with your body
- Listen to your heart
- Express your emotions through creativity and compassion

I developed this process during my years as an expressive arts therapist and refined it through my own healing path. You will be invited to slow down, to feel deeply, and to create a space for what has been waiting to emerge. Your truth, your tenderness, and your wholeness.

Before you begin, I invite you to create a small sacred corner for yourself. Light a candle, pour a warm drink, wrap yourself in a soft blanket. Let your nervous system know: I am safe to feel now. I am safe to heal.

This is your time. This is your sanctuary. And you don't have to do it perfectly. You just have to be willing to show up with love.

I'm honored to walk with you along your path.

With deep compassion,

Carla Mino

HOW TO USE THIS WORKBOOK

This workbook is your sacred space. A quiet, creative container where you can soften, feel, and heal at your own pace.

There's no need to fix yourself. You are here to remember yourself.

This journey unfolds through four parts:

1. Coming Home to the Body: reconnect with your body as a place of wisdom and safety.

2. Listening to the Heart: Discover your emotional truth and spiritual voice.

3. Expressing to Heal: Release held emotions through art, movement, and writing.

4. Integrating Love & Compassion: Embody new ways of being rooted in tenderness.

Each section includes:

- A theme and quote to center your heart.
- A guided practice (meditation, imagery, or movement)
- Journaling prompts for reflection and insight
- A creative arts invitation for emotional expression
- A gentle ritual or integration practice

Your Sacred Rhythm

There is no right way to move through this.

You can:

- Follow the workbook in order, over 4-6 weeks
- Choose one section per week and revisit as needed
- Open to whatever page your heart needs today

You might want to keep nearby:

- A pen or pencil
- Colored pencils, oil pastels, or watercolors
- Scissors and glue (for collage or symbol work)
- A candle, playlist, or object that feels grounding

Tips for Your Journey

- Set aside 20-30 minutes per session or more if your soul needs it
- Read each practice slowly, breathe between the lines
- Be gentle with what comes up. There is no rush or judgement
- Let your emotions guide your pace
- If something feels too tender, skip or pause. You can always return.

Before You Begin

Take a moment to settle into your body.

Place your hands on your heart.

Inhale.

Exhale.

Whisper to yourself:

"I am safe. I am ready. I am here."

Let this be your return to self, with love.

Creating Your Sacred Space

Before you begin, I invite you to create a quiet space that feels like a refuge. A space that reminds your heart: you are safe to feel, to rest, and to heal here.

You don't need anything fancy. What matters most is intention. This is a space to soften, reconnect, and meet yourself with love.

What to Gather?

Consider including:

- A candle or soft light to symbolize presence and warmth.
- A cozy blanket or cushion to ground and support your body
- Sacred objects such as a stone, shell, feather, photo, or a symbol that hold meaning for you.
- A journal and pen. Choose one that feels good in your hands.
- Art supplies such as colored pencils, markers, or collage materials.
- Soothing sounds. A soft playlist, singing bowl, or simply silence.
- A warm drink. Tea, cacao, or anything comforting.

Setting the Tone

You can make this space permanent or temporary.

Even if it's just a corner of your bed or your kitchen at sunrise, let it feel intentional.

Before each session:

1. Take a breath
2. Light a candle or say a prayer.
3. Place your hand on your heart.
4. Whisper **"I enter this space with love."**

Sacred Space as Ritual

Let this moment be your threshold:

- From rushing to stillness.
- From distraction to presence.
- From outside noise to inner truth.

This is beyond exercises. You are nurturing your spirit.

Let this space witness your becoming.

Creating a Sacred Space Checklist

- I lit a candle, incense, or turned on soft lighting
- I am in a quiet and safe environment
- I brought something comforting (cozy blanket, tea, essential oil)
- I gathered my Love & Compassion workbook and art supplies
- I took 3 deep breaths to settle into my body
- I repeated words of affirmation:

"I am safe. I am present. I am open to receive.

This space is sacred. I am sacred."

WHAT IS LOVE & COMPASSION?

Love and compassion are the sacred language of the soul. They are emotions we experience through healing forces that soften our pain, nourish our spirit, and reconnect us to our divine essence.

Love is presence. It is the quiet yet powerful energy that holds space for who you truly are. No judgement. No rushing. No needing to fix anything. Reminding you that you are enough as you are. It is a whispering of you are worthy, belong, and matter.

Compassion is love in action. It is the gentleness that responds to your pain with warmth, curiosity, and care. Compassion allows you to be human, to make mistakes, to rest when you are exhausted, and to begin anew as many times as needed.

The two lead you to a path of healing.

They guide you home to your body, heart, and spirit. They help you forgive yourself, hold space for your emotions, and walk with gentleness through strength.

This workbook invites you to explore love and compassion as daily practices that live in your breath, choices, relationships, and creative expression.

Love and compassion live within you.

This journey is allowing you to remember.

MY STORY: A JOURNEY THROUGH COMPASSION & REBIRTH

The Love and Compassion Formula began as a vision in 2004. Prior to this moment, during my graduate internship in marriage and family therapy, I worked with dual-diagnosis clients (severe mental health and addictions) at a psychiatric outpatient clinic. I intuitively combined traditional therapy with expressive arts and guided imagery. My clients began to heal through self-forgiveness, reframing emotions, and reconnecting with themselves. One client even asked me to record a guided meditation to continue her healing at home.

Despite my clients' progress, my use of nontraditional techniques was questioned. My clinic supervisor felt I wasn't following the standard marriage and family therapy model. Combined with a personal crisis that included my father's illness, academic overload, and burnout, I was dismissed from the program. I felt ashamed and deeply depressed. At the time, I didn't understand that my body was signaling I was not in the right place.

Eventually, I enrolled in an expressive arts therapy graduate program, where I formally studied the healing power of creativity. Along with my previous dedication to practicing Zen meditation since I was 20 years old, this led me to study compassion, forgiveness, transformation, and spiritual healing. After graduating, I worked as an expressive arts therapist with people of all ages, including celebrities/ high-profile clients at luxury rehabilitation centers and mental health care retreat programs. I presented my research and techniques at conferences and created programs still in use today.

But life took a turn. I faced loss. The death of my father and grandparents and a difficult divorce. I became my own advocate in family court and lost touch with my creative path. I shifted into education to support my daughter and tried other careers, including grant writing and editing. Some opportunities ended in disappointment and even financial hardship.

My burnout deepened and I lost confidence in my gifts. I equated my worth with performance. In 2023, after a severe illness and emotional crash, I finally surrendered. I rested, watched movies, ate slowly, journaled, and realized what rest could feel like. That simple act of slowing down began my return to self-love.

Therapy, bloodwork, and substitute teaching brought structure back into my life, but I still felt unfulfilled. I earned a certificate in business administration and explored entrepreneurship. Slowly, I began to remember who I was. A therapist helped me reconnect with my purpose and I realized I had been living the formula I created all those years ago.

Then came one final test. In excruciating physical pain, I turned inward. My body was communicating with me through pain because I had not listened to it prior to this. With the guidance of a healer, I gently placed my hands over the area and whispered, I love you. I will never abandon you. I danced slowly, listened to soothing music, spoke lovingly to my body, nourished it with healthy foods, and felt the pain eventually fade away. At that moment, I promised to treat myself with compassion and listen to my body for the rest of my life.

That experience awakened something in me. I finally felt whole, motivated, and clear. I was ready to share the Love and Compassion Formula, the very method I had once been criticized for using. It was always meant to be shared, but first I had to live it.

This workbook is that offering.

Part One

RECONNECTING WITH THE SELF

BEGIN WHERE YOU ARE: A GROUNDING PRACTICE

Before healing, clarity, or transformation is the simple yet powerful act of arriving. To begin where you are is to meet yourself honestly, tenderly and without judgement.

It's the moment you say, *I am dedicated to my journey of compassion.*

Grounding is the practice of returning to your body and breath. It brings you out of the swirling thoughts of the mind and into the quiet truth of the present moment. It reminds you that you are safe right where you are.

You don't have to feel ready. All that you need is your willingness to pause, feel your feet on the floor, and connect with the wisdom within you.

This practice is your anchor. It gently holds you as you explore the love and compassion one breath and one moment at a time.

Guided Grounding Exercise

You may sit or lie down in a comfortable position. Allow your hands to rest gently on your lap or heart.

1. Close your eyes (if you feel safe to do so) and take a slow, deep breath in through your nose.

   Let it fill your belly...then exhale slowly through your mouth.

2. Take two more deep breaths at your own pace.

   With each exhale, release a little tension.

3. Bring your attention to your feet.

   Feel them resting on the floor or surface below you. Imagine roots extending down into the Earth as strong, steady, and embracing you.

4. Move your awareness up through your legs, hips, and spine.

   Notice where your body is touching the earth, a chair, a bed, or any point of contact.

   Breathe into those places. Let your body feel supported.

5. Place one hand on your heart and one on your belly.

   As you breathe, say gently to yourself (aloud or silently)

"I am here. I am safe. I am allowed to slow down."

6. Stay in this stillness for a few moments. You may notice sensations, emotions, or thoughts arise, let them move through the clouds in the sky.

7. When you are ready, open your eyes softly. Wiggle your fingers and toes.

Offer yourself a gentle smile.

You have arrived.

THE BODY SPEAKS: SOMATIC CHECK-INS

Where I Am Today

A quiet moment to check in with yourself, honestly, and gently.

Date: _________________

Time of day: ______________

Location or setting: ____

Body

- How does my body feel right now?

(Tight, tired, restless, calm, open, heavy, energized...)

____

____

____

____

____

____

____

- Where am I holding tension or emotion in my body?

____

____

____

____

- What is one kind thing I can offer my body today?

____

____

____

____

Heart

- What emotions are present right now?

(You can circle or write: anxious, grateful, sad, hopeful, numb, curious...)

____

____

____

____

- Is there a message my heart is whispering?

____

____

____

____

- What do I need most emotionally today?

____

____

____

____

Spirit

- Do I feel connected or disconnected from myself today?

____

____

____

____

- What might help me feel more spiritually supported?

(Rest, prayer, nature, art, silence, movement...)

____

____

____

____

____

____

A gentle Affirmation or prayer for this moment

I am

____

____

____

____

____

You might close your check-in with a breath, a stretch, or a small ritual like lighting a candle or placing your hand on your heart.

GUIDED IMAGERY & STILLNESS PRACTICE

Opening a Sacred Inner Space

Guided imagery is a gentle, intuitive way to access the wisdom of your inner world. When we soften into stillness, we open the doorway to a sacred space within us. A place where healing images, memories, and truths begin to arise through sensing and feeling.

Stillness is about presence. It's a quiet space where your nervous system can relax, your breath can deepen, and your body can feel safe enough to speak.

In this chapter, you will be invited to enter a calm, inner space using imagery and imagination. Whether you are guided to a peaceful meadow, a healing light, or a sacred memory, allow your experience to unfold without force. Your body and spirit already know what you need.

This practice is about trusting that what arises in stillness is worthy of being heard. It is a loving conversation between your inner self and your soul.

JOURNAL PROMPTS: LISTENING TO YOUR BODY'S NEEDS

When we are burned out, overwhelmed, or in pain, the body often becomes a place we ignore, abandon, or try to push through. But your body is not the enemy. It is your first home, your shelter, your compass, and your messenger.

This part of your journey is about gently returning to your body. It's about listening, honoring, and reconnecting. When we come back to the body with love, we begin to rewire safety, presence, and compassion from the inside out.

Journal Prompts

What is my current relationship with my body?

____

____

____

____

____

____

____

What have I believed about my body during stress or trauma?

____

____

____

____

____

How would I like to begin relating to my body differently?

____

____

____

____

____

What does my body need to feel safe, heard or honored?

____

____

____

____

REFLECTION PAGE: MY BODY WISDOM

Why the Body Matters

The body remembers everything. Our stories, our survival, our joy, and our grief. It holds tension when we are afraid, softens when we feel safe, and speaks through symptoms when something is unspoken.

By tuning into the body, we begin to:

- Recognize where we carry stress or emotion.
- Soften our nervous system.
- Reclaim our ability to feel and rest.
- Create a safe foundation for deeper healing.

Practice: Gentle Body Awareness

Find a quiet place and take 5 slow breaths.

Close your eyes.

Place one hand on your heart and the other on your belly.

Ask yourself...

Where do I feel grounded?

Where do I feel tight or tender?

What is one sensation I notice without judgement?

Just observe. There is no need to change anything. Just be with what is present right now.

Whisper to yourself:

"I am allowed to take up space. I hold wisdom in my body."

Journal Your Reflections

____

____

____

____

____

____

____

____

____

Creative Invitation:

My Body as Sacred

Create a body map using a silhouette of your body.

Draw your body and mark the places where you feel...

Emotion

Numbness

Energy

Longing

Peace

Use colors, symbols, or words to represent the feelings.

You may also write a short note to your body. Take three deep breaths and connect with your body.

Dear body,

I'm listening now. Tell me about how you are doing.

____

____

____

____

____

____

____

____

____

____

____

____

____

Integration Ritual:

Bless Your Body

Before bed or after a bath, gently slather lotion or oil on your body. As you touch each part, whisper:

Thank you feet for carrying me.
Thank you shoulders for holding so much.
Thank you breath for giving me life.
Thank you organs for working properly.

Let this be a loving act of returning home.

Part Two

EXPRESSIVE ARTS FOR HEALING

THE POWER OF
CREATIVE EXPRESSION

Expression is how emotions move through us. When we don't have a safe way to release, emotions can get stuck in the body, the heart, the breath. But when we let ourselves express ourselves with color, words, sound, or movement, we begin to open again.

In this part, you will gently allow what is inside to come forward, without judgement or needing to be perfect. Don't expect yourself to be an artist with perfect techniques. It's about being honest.

You are allowed to make a mess. You are allowed to color outside the lines. You are allowed to create beauty. You are allowed to feel.

Why Expression Matters

Expressive healing lets your truth flow. It...

Releases emotion safely.

Bypasses overthinking.

Unlocks intuition.

Transforms pain into meaning.

Helps you feel acknowledged.

Practice: 10 minute Expressive Release

Set a timer for 10 minutes. Choose one method:

Scribble with crayons or markers.

Free to write whatever comes to mind.

Tear and collage images from old magazines.

Move your body to music with eyes closed.

Paint or draw using only color and shapes.

Let go of the outcome. Follow your feelings. Express, instead of impress.

There is no wrong or right way to create.

Express Yourself:

Draw Your Experience:

Creative Invitation:

My Healing Colors

Create an abstract piece using colors that represent your emotional state.

Ask...

What color is my sadness?____

What color is my joy? ____

What shape does my impatience take?____________________________________

What shape does courage take?____

Use watercolor, oil pastels, or anything soft and fluid. When you are finished, give it a title. You can use the space below if using pastels, coloring pencils, and marker or another piece of paper if using watercolor or paint.

Title: ____

Integration Ritual:

Witness Your Expression

When you are done, take a pause. Look at what you created. Gently say aloud:

This is a part of me.

I see you.

Thank you for showing up for me.

Then place or hang the artwork somewhere meaningful. Let it be your sacred art.

Reflections:

____

____

____

____

____

____

____

____

____

DRAWING: SYMBOLS OF INNER PEACE

Drawing invites you to express what words cannot. Inner calm is reflected by shapes, symbols, and colors. In this practice, you will create visual representations of peace as it lives in your body, spirit, or imagination.

Creative Prompt:

If peace lived in a shape, color, or symbol...what would it look like?

Close your eyes and take a few deep breaths. Invite an image, color, or symbol to arise. Choose one that represents peace for you today. Don't overthink it. Let your hand move freely and allow the image to form naturally.

Use the space below to draw or doodle your symbol of inner peace.

POETRY: WRITING FROM THE HEART

Why the Heart Matters

The heart is the bridge between the body and the soul. When we listen to it, we:

- Connect to our inner wisdom.
- Access emotion safely and compassionately.
- Clarify what matters most to us.
- Begin to feel seen, by ourselves.

You don't have to solve everything. You just have to listen.

Practice: The Hand to Heart Pause

Sit somewhere quiet. Place one or both hands over your heart. Close your eyes.

Ask gently the questions below. Breathe slowly. Don't rush the answer. Trust the silence.

What am I feeling right now?

____

____

____

____

____

What does my heart want to say?

____

____

____

____

____

What does my heart need most?

Say this affirmation...

I am safe to feel what is arising within me.

Journal Prompt

If my heart had a voice, what would it say today?

What is my heart tired of holding?

What does my heart long to receive more of?

What breaks my heart and what opens it?

Creative Invitation:

Love Letter to Your Heart

Write a letter to your heart as if it were a dear friend. Let it be raw, poetic, or messy.

You might begin with...

> *Dear Heart, I'm sorry I haven't always listened...*
> *Thank you for still beating, even when...*
> *I want to learn how to care for you like...*

Use watercolors, collage, or ink if you would like to decorate it.

Dear Heart,

Love,

Poetry Prompt:

Write a poem that begins with the words:

In the quiet of my heart...

Let your heart speak without editing or explanation.

It might come out as a whisper, a prayer or a declaration. Trust its rhythm.

There is no right way to write this. Honor your truth, as it wants to be heard today.

Title of Poem: ____

In the quiet of my heart, ____

____

____

____

____

____

____

____

____

____

____

MOVEMENT: RELEASING EMOTION THROUGH THE BODY

Your body remembers everything. It holds the weight of unspoken emotions, tension from old stories, and the energy of experiences you may not even have words for. Movement is a powerful way to gently release what your body no longer needs without forcing, fixing, or explaining.

This practice is about allowing your body to move in ways that feel freeing, grounding, and true. Whether it is a slow sway, a deep stretch, or a trembling release. Every motion is a message of love.

Practice

1. Put on gentle music or sit in silence.
2. Close your eyes and take 3 deep breaths.
3. Ask your body...*What do you need to release today?*
4. Begin moving softly, slowly, or with intensity. However your body asks.
5. Let your body lead. Let your breath follow. Let your mind rest.

Creative Invitation

After your movement, take a few moments to reflect.

- What did your body release?

- What did it express through movement?

- Create a drawing, freewrite, or a short poem to honor what moved through you.

This is your sacred release. Let it be enough.

Integration Ritual: Sacred Listening Walk

Go outside or a quiet space without a destination. Walk slowly as if your heart were guiding your feet. With each step, repeat kindly to yourself:

I'm listening.

I'm here.

I'm open.

What do you want to share with me?

Let your heart lead, even if it's only to stillness.

Reflections from your walk:

____

____

____

____

____

____

____

____

____

____

MUSIC AND SOUND:
A SOOTHING COMPANION

Music is one of the most ancient forms of emotional alchemy. It bypasses the mind and speaks directly to the heart, carrying with it frequencies that can calm, awaken, soften or uplift. In moments when words fail, sound becomes a sacred companion. It offers comfort, surrendering, and remembrance.

Whether it's a soft instrumental piece, a favorite song from childhood, or the sound of ocean waves, music has the power to bring you back to yourself. You can hum, chant, drum, or simply listen. Let sound move through your body gently, like warm water, loosening what's tight and filling what feels empty.

This practice is about feeling. Let the music guide your breath. Let it open a doorway to healing.

Practice: Listening with the Heart

1. Choose a piece of music or sound that feels calming, uplifting, or emotionally resonant.

   (Instrumentals, nature sounds, sacred music, or personal favorites all work beautifully.)

2. Find a quiet space and close your eyes. Breathe slowly and listen with your heart.

   Ask yourself... *What feeling does this sound stir in me?*

3. Allow any memories, emotions, or images to arise without judgment.

4. Stay with the sound for 5-10 minutes. Let it wash over you and embrace you.

Sound Reflection Prompt:

What sounds bring your soul peace?

____

Think of a song, melody, or natural sound that helps you feel calm, safe, or seen.

Close your eyes, play or imagine it, and allow yourself to breathe with it.

What feelings does this sound awaken in me?

____

____

____

____

What does my body do when I listen?

____

____

____

____

If this sound could speak, what message would it carry for me today?

____

____

____

____

Use the space below to journal, draw, or simply sit in silence with your sound companion.

Creative Invitation

Translate Sound into Expression. After your sound experience, take a moment to reflect or create.

Draw or paint what the music felt like in color, shape, or energy.

Write a few lines of poetry beginning with

The music reminded me...

____

____

____

____

____

What emotions surfaced?

____

____

____

____

What did I need to hear?

____

____

____

____

Allow your creative response to give form to what your soul felt. Draw your experience.

Integration: Let the Silence Hold you

When the music ends, take three deep breaths in silence.

Ask yourself...

What do I feel now that I didn't before?

____

____

____

____

How did sound shift or soothe something inside me?

____

____

____

____

What kind of sound will invite more often into my healing space?

____

____

____

Close by placing your hands on your heart and simply saying...

"Thank you."

To the sound. To yourself. To this moment.

JOURNALING: WHAT I FEEL, WHAT I RELEASE

Emotions are messengers. They rise up to speak to you, ask for your presence, your breath, and your compassion. In this space you are invited to slow down, name what you are feeling, and gently release what no longer serves your body or spirit.

Your emotions hold wisdom, but sometimes they get buried beneath overthinking, pressure, or silence. Journaling helps you slow down and listen. To name what is present, to release what you no longer need, and to gently return to yourself with more compassion and clarity.

There is no emotion too big or too small to bring here. Every tear, every frustration, every joy is welcome.

Be honest with your feelings. Make space for the truth of your experience and trust that release is part of the healing.

Let this be a space where you feel safe to explore your inner world without judgement, just presence, and love.

Practice: Honoring What is Real

1. Find a quiet, nurturing space.
2. Take three slow breaths and ask yourself

What do I feel right now without needing to change it?

1. Begin writing freely. Let your pen move without filtering or fixing. Use this prompt:

Right now, I feel…

____

____

____

____

____

____

____

2. After a few minutes, shift into release by asking…
What can I lovingly let go of today?

____

____

____

____

____

____

____

3. Pause when you feel complete. Take a breath and honor your courage.

Prompts:

1. What emotion is present in me right now and where do I feel it in my body?
(Close your eyes and scan your body with compassion.)

z____

____

____

—

2. If this emotion had a voice, what would it say?

____

____

____

____

3. What do I need to feel safe enough to let this go or let it be here gently held?

____

____

____

____

4. What am I ready to release from my heart today?

____

____

____

____

____

5. What would it feel like to forgive myself or someone else just a little more?

____

____

____

____

____

6. When I think of peace, what image, word, or sensation comes to mind?
(Let this be your anchor as you move forward.)

____

____

____

____

Creative Invitation: Express What Was Set Free

After journaling, choose a creative way to express what you let go of...

- Tear up or safely burn a page (if it feels right and safe) to symbolize release.
- Create a simple drawing or collage of the feeling as it leaves your body.
- Write a short, gentle affirmation like..

"I honor what I felt and I welcome peace."

Let your creativity offer closure, softness, and beauty.

(Below is your sacred space to create or/and write).

Integration: What Remains, What Is Opening

Sit in stillness for a moment and ask...

What remains now that I've expressed and released?

____

____

____

____

____

____

What am I making space for?

____

____

____

____

____

____

What does my heart need as I move forward today?

____

____

____

____

____

____

____

____

____

____

Write down one supportive word or phrase that you can carry with you.

____

Let it be a reminder that what you feel is valid and what you release is sacred.

REFLECTIONS: MY ARTISTIC VOICE

Your artistic voice is the soul's language expressed through color, sound, words, movement, and feeling. These prompts invite you to reflect on how your creativity is part of your healing and how it longs to be heard.

Practice: Listening to Your Creative Soul

You don't need to be a trained artist to have an artistic voice. Your voice already lives in the way you see, feel, express, and make meaning. This practice is about listening to the part of you that wants to speak through image, rhythm, color, and story.

Don't worry about impressing others. Your artistic voice is expressing what is real and sacred within you.

1. Take a few moments to breathe and ground yourself.
2. Reflect on a moment in your journey where creativity helped you feel seen, hearts, or soothed.
3. Ask yourself...

What does my artistic voice sound like? Look like? Feel like?

Let your memory and emotions guide you. Write freely or begin to sketch something abstract that represents your creative truth.

Write

Sketch

Journal Prompts:

1. What creative expression felt most natural to me during this journey and why?

____

____

____

____

2. When I create without judgement, what parts of me come alive?

____

____

____

____

____

3. What have I discovered about myself through drawing, movement, writing, or sound?

____

____

____

____

4. If my inner artist had a message for me, what would it say?

____

____

____

____

____

____

____

5. How can I honor and nurture my creativity in daily life, even in small ways?

____

____

____

____

____

____

Creative Invitation: Meet Your Artist Within

Choose a medium. Whether it's writing, collage, movement, doodling, or color. Create something that feels like a message from your inner artist. It could be...

- A symbol that represents your creative spirit.
- A few lines of poetry that begin with "My voice says..."
- A free-flow sketch or abstract image of your energy in this moment.

Let your hand move without judgement. You are making space for you.

Creative Integration: Claiming Your Voice

After you have created, sit with your work for a moment. Place your hand on your heart and ask...

What did I learn about myself through this?

____

____

____

____

____

____

What do I want to express more of in my life?

____

____

____

____

____

____

How can I honor my artistic voice beyond this page?

____

____

____

____

____

____

Write a short reflection or affirmation to carry with you.

"My voice is sacred. I express with love, honesty, and freedom"

____

____

____

____

____

____

____

Part Three

HEART CENTERED HEALING

If your body is your ground, then your heart is your guide. Beneath the noise of doubt, stress or survival, your heart holds truth. It knows your longing. It knows what hurts. It knows what matters most.

In this part of your journey, you will slow down to meet your heart. Just as it is. No pushing, no fixing. Just presence. Here, we begin to honor what you truly feel, what you deeply need, and what your soul longs to say.

UNDERSTANDING COMPASSION

Compassion is more than kindness. It is a sacred presence that says, I see your pain and I choose to be present with you. It invites us to witness ourselves and others with softness without judgement. It holds a space with love. True compassion begins within: when we stop criticizing our flaws, slow down when we are tired, and offer grace when we are learning. It is a daily practice of returning to the heart. We remember that healing happens through gentleness. In this chapter, you are invited to explore what it means to live compassionately with your body, emotions, and spirit.

Reflection Prompts:

1. What does compassion mean to me? How do I live and relate to myself and others?

____

____

____

____

____

____

____

2. When was the last time I offered true compassion to myself? What did it look or feel like?

____

____

____

____

____

____

____

3. What makes it hard for me to be compassionate toward myself at times? What helps me soften?

____

____

____

____

____

____

4. How does compassion feel different from judgement, control, or fixing?

____

____

____

____

____

____

5. What would it sound like if I spoke to myself with the voice of someone who deeply loves me?

(Write a few lines in that voice.)

____

____

____

____

____

____

____

6. Who in my life has modeled compassion for me? And what did I learn from them?

Mini Meditation: A Moment of Self-Compassion

Sit comfortably. Place your hand over your heart or another area that needs love.

Take a slow, deep breath.

As you exhale, silently say to yourself..

May I be gentle with myself.

Breathe.

May I offer myself love and understanding.

Breathe.

May I remember I am doing the best I can.

Stay here for a few moments. Let the warmth of your hand and breath anchor you.

There is nothing to fix.

Only the cradling of your heart.

FORGIVENESS AS A PRACTICE

Forgiveness is a practice of returning to the heart again and again. It's the quiet willingness to release the pain we have carried and not to forget or excuse what happened. It is to set ourselves free. True forgiveness begins with compassion. It's forgiving the parts of us that hurt, didn't know better, and for the weight we have held in silence.

Sometimes, forgiveness takes time. It comes through tears, letters never sent, or gentle prayers whispered in solitude. Choosing to heal the past and not pretending the past didn't happen is forgiveness.

Each act of forgiveness is a step toward lightness, a movement back to wholeness.

You are not weak for forgiving. You are strong for loving yourself enough to let go.

Practice: A Soft Opening to Forgiveness

Forgiveness is about choosing to release the emotional weight we carry so we can return to peace within ourselves. This practice invites you to begin where you are with honesty, softness, and grace. You do not need to rush. Forgiveness is a journey, not a destination.

1. Find a quiet space and place your hand on your heart. Take three slow breaths.
2. Gently bring to mind a situation, a person, or part of yourself that still holds pain. Don't force anything. Just notice what arises.
3. Ask yourself...

What am I holding onto here?

How has this been affecting my spirit or body?

1. Write freely for 5-10 minutes. Allow your truth to come through without judgement.

I'm still hurting because

____

____

____

____

____

____

A part of me is ready to release

Forgiveness, to me, means

2. When you feel ready, close your eyes and say silently or aloud...

I offer myself compassion as I open to forgiveness.

3. End with a gesture of care by placing your hands together in prayer, hug yourself, or place both hands over your heart.

Reflection Prompts

1. Who or what am I ready to forgive, even if only a little today?

(This might include yourself.)

____

____

____

____

____

____

____

____

____

____

2. What emotions come up when I think about forgiveness?

(Let them move through without rushing.)

____

____

____

____

____

____

____

3. What does my heart need in order to soften and release what it's been holding?

____

____

____

____

____

____

____

4. Finish this sentence.

I am willing to forgive because...

5. Write a compassionate letter to yourself or someone else. (Don't send the letter. Just allow the words to come through.)

Dear______________________________________,

____

____

____

____

____

____

____

____

____

____

____

____

Love,

____

Creative Invitation: Expressing the Shift

Let your hands speak what your heart is feeling.

Choose one of the following creative invitations...

- Draw or paint what forgiveness feels like in color or shape
- Create a symbol of emotional release. It could be a feather, an open door, an ocean wave
- Write a letter to the person or part of you that you are forgiving. No need to send it. Just express what you feel.

Art is not judging you. Art is healing you.

Creative Integration: Honoring the Opening

As you close this practice, reflect on what forgiveness awakened or softened in you.

Reflect on the following...

What did I create space for today?

____

____

____

____

____

____

What am I ready to let go of, even a little?

____

____

____

____

____

____

How can I offer myself compassion as I continue to heal?

____

____

____

____

____

____

Write one affirmation or intention to carry forward...

I forgive my freedom.

I choose peace.

Each day, I return to love.

____

____

____

____

____

____

Allow your becoming to blossom.

REBIRTH THROUGH SELF-LOVE

Rebirth happens quietly, often after we think we have lost everything. It's in the moments we choose to rest instead of push, to nourish instead of criticize, to listen to ourselves with tenderness instead of judgement. Self-love is the soil from which our healing blooms. It is the gentle foundation for your transformation.

To love yourself is to say...

I am worthy of care. I am allowed to begin again.

Every time you choose kindness toward yourself, you are rewriting a story that once said you had to earn love.

You don't have to earn love. You are love.

Rebirth through self-love is a return to who you are underneath it all. Radiant, whole, and deeply enough.

Reflection Prompts:

1. What part of me feels ready to be seen, nurtured, or reclaimed?

____

____

____

____

2. What would it look like to begin again with grace instead of pressure?

____

____

____

____

3. How can I offer love to myself through a small daily act of care?

____

____

____

____

4. What limiting belief about myself am I ready to shed?

____

____

____

____

____

____

____

5. Write a love note to the version of you who is emerging. Honor her courage, her gentleness, and her strength.

____

____

____

____

____

____

____

JOURNAL PROMPTS: LETTING GO, LETTING IN

Letting go is an act of trust. Letting in is an act of love.

Together, they create space to release what no longer serves you and welcome what your spirit truly needs.

You are invited here to gently loosen your grip on old patterns, beliefs, or burdens. Not all at once. Just enough to breathe.

And as you breathe, ask yourself...

What am I ready to welcome?

These prompts are your doorway into that sacred exchange of release and renewal.

Prompts

1. What am I holding onto that is weighing me down or keeping me small?

____

____

____

____

2. What fear or story am I ready to lay down, even if just for today?

____

____

____

____

3. What qualities, feelings, or beliefs do I long to invite into my life now?

____

____

____

____

4. If I released this weight, how might I feel emotionally, physically, spiritually?

____

____

____

____

____

____

5. What would it feel like to live more open, more free, more connected to who I truly am?

____

____

____

____

____

____

REFLECTION PAGE:
A COMPASSIONATE SELF

This page is an offering to your most loving self. The version of you that speaks with kindness, moves with grace, and believes in her own worth.

Take a moment to witness her. She's already inside you.

Reflection

Use the space below to write, draw, or affirm your compassionate self.

I see the woman I'm becoming and she is

____

____

____

____

____

____

____

____

My compassionate self tells me

____

____

____

____

____

____

I am learning to love myself even when

____

____

____

____

____

Space to Sketch/ Draw

Affirmations

____

Part Four

30 DAYS OF THE LOVE & COMPASSION FORMULA

HOW TO USE THE 30-DAY PRACTICE OF THE LOVE AND COMPASSION FORMULA

This 30-day journey is an invitation to reconnect with your inner world. Gently, honestly, and with deep compassion. Each day, you will engage with one simple practice inspired by the Love and Compassion Formula, a healing process rooted in presence, creativity, emotional awareness, and self-love.

You don't need to have it all figured out. You don't need to be "healed" to begin. You simply begin where you are. With a breath, a page, and a pause.

How to Use This Practice

- Set aside sacred time each day. Even just 10-20 minutes for your practice. Morning or evening, whatever feels most natural to you.

- Each day offers a gentle prompt or expression invitation.

- Follow the flow of what is offered, but feel free to adapt it to what you need. Some days you may write. Some days you may rest. Yes! Resting is part of your love and compassion practice.

- Keep a compassionate heart toward yourself. If you miss a day, return with love, not guilt. The formula is about softening, not perfection.

- At the end of each week, reflect on what's shifting. Whether it is emotionally, spiritually, or energetically. Let the insights come naturally.

Don't see this as a checklist. This is not proving you are perfect. It's a healing rhythm to build a deeper relationship with yourself through trust, tenderness, and creative expression.

Your heart already knows the way. This practice helps you listen.

Week 1: Coming Home to Your Body

Day 1. What is your body asking for today and how can you gently respond?

Day 2. Place your hand on your heart. What does it want you to know right now?

Day 3. How does safety feel in your body? Describe it.

Day 4. In what ways can you offer kindness to your physical self?

Day 5. Reflect on a moment when your body felt truly alive. What were you doing?

Day 6. What part of your body needs compassion today? Write a loving note to it.

Day 7. Practice stillness. What arises in the silence?

Week 2: Listening to Your Heart

Day 8. What does your heart long for today?

____

____

____

____

____

____

____

____

____

____

____

____

____

Day 9. Write a letter of forgiveness to yourself or someone else.

Day 10. What emotions are living in your chest right now? Name them gently.

Day 11. How do you define self-love in this season of your life?

Day 12. Recall a time you felt deeply loved. What made it feel safe?

Day 13. What fear is ready to be met with love?

Day 14. Finish this sentence: *If I truly listened to my heart, I would...*

Week 3: Releasing & Rebirthing

Day 15. What belief or story are you ready to release?

Day 16. Where in your life are you holding on too tightly?

Day 17. What would it feel like to trust your healing path completely?

Day 18. Imagine your healing as a rebirth. What is being born within you?

Day 19. What are you grieving and what would it look like to grieve with compassion?

Day 20. Describe a time when you surprised yourself with your strength.

Day 21. What would it feel like to be free?

Week 4: Creating with Soul

Day 22. What would your inner child create if there were no limits?

Day 23. Create a symbol or image that represents your healing journey.

Day 24. What colors express your emotions today? Why?

Day 25. What do you want your life to feel like in six months?

Day 26. If your voice mattered deeply, what would you say?

Day 27. What message do you want to leave behind with your art or words?

Day 28. What beauty is already within you waiting to be expressed?

Week 5: Living the Formula

Day 29. What is one compassionate habit you would like to cultivate daily?

Final Reflection

Day 30. What would it look like to live your life with sacred softness, grace, and love?

Part Five

INTEGRATION & VISIONING

You have listened to your body.

You have honored your heart.

You have expressed what was waiting to be seen.

Now, we begin to integrate. Integration is weaving love and compassion into the way you live, speak to you

Why Integration Matters

Without integration, healing can feel like a temporary relief.

But with integration, transformation becomes sustainable.

It allows you to:

- Ground your emotional shifts in daily rituals.
- Speak more kindly to yourself.
- Notice when old wounds arise and meet them differently.
- Walk through life from a place of wholeness not survival.

Practice: Daily Compassion Ritual

Choose a time each day to offer yourself a simple act of love. **Schedule** it if that helps you remember.

Monday: _____:______ AM/PM

Tuesday: _____:______ AM/PM

Wednesday: _____:______ AM/PM

Thursday: _____:______ AM/PM

Friday: _____:______ AM/PM

Saturday: _____:______ AM/PM

Sunday: _____:______ AM/PM

Here are a few ways to integrate compassion daily

Place your hand over your heart and whisper:

"I'm proud of you."

Write one loving truth on a sticky note.

"You are enough."

And place it where you will see it.

A bathroom mirror, refrigerator, etc.

Gently stretch or touch your body with kindness.

Bless your food or water before you eat.

Sit in silence and breathe deeply for one full minute.

Start small. Repeat often.

Journal Prompt

What has shifted in me through this journey so far?

____

____

____

____

____

____

How do I speak to myself now compared to before?

____

____

____

____

____

____

What does love in action look like in my daily life?

____

____

____

____

____

____

____

____

What are 3 practices I want to continue moving forward?

1. ____

____

2. ____

____

3. ____

____

Creative Invitation: My Compassion Toolkit

Design a visual page called your "Compassion Toolkit."

Include:

Words or phrases that comfort you.

Rituals that bring peace.

Movement or art practices you love.

People or spaces that feel safe.

Notes to self, mantras, reminders.

Use collage, markers, or even photos. Let it be a map you can return to when you feel lost.

My Compassion Toolkit

Integration Ritual: Mirror Blessing

Stand in front of a mirror. Look into your own eyes.

Take a breath and say:

"I am whole. I am becoming."

"I am worthy of love, especially from myself."

"Thank you for staying."

Let this be your daily blessing. Your beginning again.

Reflection:

____

____

____

____

____

____

____

____

____

CLOSING:
A RETURN TO YOURSELF

If you have come this far, I want you to know:

You have already healed in ways you may not yet fully see.

You have chosen to listen, to feel, to express, and to love yourself more deeply. To have compassion for yourself is to love yourself.

This is the beginning of living from a place of sacred compassion.

Allow the tools in this workbook live on your shelf or altar as a companion. Something you can return to whenever you forget, whenever you need to be reminded:

You are whole. You are sacred. You are worthy of softness and care.

FINAL REFLECTION:
A LOVE LETTER TO MYSELF

Take some quiet time to reflect on your journey. Then, write a love letter to yourself.

"Dear ____________________(your name),

I'm so proud of the way you _________________"

You may include:

What you have discovered

What you are letting go of

What you are reclaiming

What promises you want to make to yourself

This letter can be kept in your journal, tucked into a drawer, or sealed and opened in a year.

Date: _____/_____/__________

Dear____,

____

____

____

____

____

____

____

____

____

____

____

____

____

____

____

____

Love,

Sacred Closure Ritual

Light a candle, sit in a cozy spot, or under the sky. Gently say aloud or write in your journal:

> ***I am not the pain I have carried.***
> ***I am not the past that shaped me.***
> ***I am the love that continues.***
> ***I am the compassion that returns.***

Place your hand over your heart. Breathe. Smile softly. Let this be your closing prayer.

Reflections

____

____

____

____

____

____

____

____

____

Keep Going

If this workbook has touched you, remember:

You can always return to any section at any time.

Healing is not linear, it is circular, gentle, and sacred.

You are never alone on this path.

Your love matters. Your softness is strength.

And you are deeply, deeply worthy of everything good for yourself to move through the world.

This is where softness becomes strength.

Where awareness becomes a practice.

Where healing becomes a way of being.

Create Your Own Love & Compassion Formula

You have spent the past 30 days connecting with your emotions, listening to your body, expressing your truth, and softening into self-love. Now it's time to gather what resonated most deeply and create a personal version of the Love and Compassion Formula that reflects you.

There's no right or wrong way. Your formula might include journaling, prayer, dancing, drawing, meditation, or walking in nature. It might begin with breathwork and end with music. What matters is that it feels like home. A sacred rhythm that supports your healing and helps you return to yourself when life feels overwhelming.

Use the space below to write or sketch the steps, elements, or practices that feel meaningful for your healing journey. This is your heart's wisdom crafted with intention, shaped by experience, and guided by love.

My Personal Love & Compassion Formula

A gentle space to gather the practices that bring me home to myself.

Step 1: My Opening Practice

What helps me ground, arrive, or open my heart?

- Deep Breath
- Soft Music
- Prayer
- Nature
- Stillness

My practice:

____

____

____

____

____

____

____

____

Step 2: What I Want to Feel or Explore

What helps me notice or connect with what I'm feeling?

- Journaling
- Body Scan
- Poetry
- Movement
- Music

Today, I am connecting with...

____

____

____

____

____

____

____

____

____

____

____

Step 3: What I Want to Release

How do I let go or soften what's heavy?

- Tears
- Dance
- Quiet
- Drawing
- Forgiveness
- My Voice
- Painting
- Writing
- Journaling
- Movement
- Sound

My practice:

____

____

____

____

____

____

____

____

4. How I Create Safety and Support

What helps me feel grounded and safe?

- Sacred Space
- Soothing Music
- Cozy Blanket

My practice:

____

____

____

____

____

____

____

____

____

____

____

5. My Compassionate Reflection

What I learned, felt, or noticed with love..

6. My Closing Ritual

How do I end with peace or gratitude?

- Blessing
- Self-hug
- Quiet Prayer
- Hand over my heart

My practice:

____

____

____

____

____

____

____

____

____

____

____

My Body Care Promise

I promise to be grateful for my body. I love you and I will take care of each of my organs from head to toe. I will nourish you with healthy food, soothing music, positive images, speak kindly, surround myself in a nurturing environment to feed my soul with gentleness. I forgive myself for neglecting you. I will comfort you. I promise to always listen to you.

Letters to My Past, Present, and Future Self

Write a letter to your past, present, and future self:

Dear Past Self,

____

____

____

____

____

Love,

____

Dear Present Self,

____

____

____

____

____

Love,

____

Dear Future Self,

Love,

Vision Pages (collage, doodles, poetry)

Use this page to express your inner world through collage, doodles, and poetry. Allow your soul to speak in images, colors, and words.

CLOSING THOUGHTS

Thank you for walking this sacred path with me.

This workbook was born from my own healing, shaped by years of learning how to listen to my body, forgive myself, and return to love again and again. My hope is that these pages helped you feel held, seen, and gently guided back to your own wisdom.

May you continue to practice self-compassion in moments of pain, as well as daily acts of devotion.

Remember that your gentleness is strength. Your body is wise. Your emotions are sacred messengers.

Above all, may you know that you are never alone on this journey.

You are worthy. You are loved. And you are already whole.

With gentleness and gratitude,

Carla Mino, M.A.

FINAL PAGES

NOTES

Use this space to capture any reflections, inspirations, quotes, ideas, or personal reminders that arise throughout your journey:

Resources for Your Journey
&
Acknowledgements

RESOURCES

You are not alone on this sacred path of healing and self-love. Below are some gentle companions (books, practices, and spaces) that may support your continued journey with grace.

Books That Gently Guide

The Mindful Self-Compassion Workbook by Dr. Kristin Neff

The Four Loves by C.S. Lewis

The Armor of God by Priscilla Shirer

Meant For Good by Megan Fate Marshman

When Strivings Cease by Ruth Chou Simons

The Creative Connection: Expressive Arts As Healing by Natalie Rogers

Gentle Support & Next Steps

Visit www.carlamino.com for free resources, soulful offerings, and updates

Book a 1:1 Compassion Coaching Session

Join the email circle for quiet reflections, spiritual prompts, and monthly love notes

Creative Healing Tools

A journal, colored pencils, or watercolors for expressive exploration

Movement practices such as qigong, dance, or intuitive stretching

A playlist of music that makes you feel held, seen, and free

If You Need More Support

If you are in emotional distress please consider reaching out to a mental health professional or calling a local support line. You are worthy of care.

ACKNOWLEDGEMENTS

This workbook was created from a place of healing, love, and devotion. To every woman who has ever felt overwhelmed, burnt out, or disconnected from herself, this is for you. May it guide you back home to your heart.

To my daughter, who embodies love, and to my mother, who shows loving strength in action. Your presence is my anchor and my inspiration. Thank you for being part of my journey of healing generational patterns. May my path of self-love and inner peace continue with the future generations.

To my dearest friends, Cora Lewis and Mark Lonier, thank you for being the sister and brother I always wished for. To my mentor, Susan Hough, and healer Karl Ardo, thank you for your gentle compassionate guidance. To my massage therapist Mandy Holden, and the Co-Op Pilates Studio, thank you for providing a sacred space for healing my body. And to my therapists , Dr. Nakju Lee and Dr. Shoura Khatibloo, thank you for your compassion and for reminding me of my power.

Above all, thank you God for the grace, vision, and strength to create and serve with love.

In gratitude,

Carla Mino

ABOUT THE AUTHOR

Carla Mino is a poet, storyteller, and guide for women on the path to healing and self-reclamation. With a background in meditation, expressive arts therapy, and over twenty years of clinical experience supporting clients ranging from creatives to those navigating trauma, burnout, and emotional overwhelm, she brings a deeply intuitive and compassionate approach to inner work.

Born in Lima, Peru, and shaped by both ancestral wisdom and sacred softness of feminine healing, her work bridges the soul, the senses, and the creative spirit. She believes in healing as a homecoming. A return to the truth that we are already whole, already worthy, and already loved.

Through writing, sacred journaling spaces, and soulful offerings, she helps women reconnect with their bodies, honor their emotions, and express their truth through beauty and gentleness. Her work is rooted in spiritual insight, the power of creativity, and the belief that gentleness is a strength.

When she is not writing or guiding others, you will find her wrapped in a soft blanket, sipping warm tea, admiring the birdsong, connecting with the sun, or walking slowly under the trees. Always listening for the next whisper of the heart.

Connect with her:
Website: www.carlamino.com
Email: hellometamorphoziz@gmail.com

www.ingramcontent.com/pod-product-compliance
Lightning Source LLC
Chambersburg PA
CBHW040206110726
48005CB00019B/2919